Pairs of Poems

Pairing poems about similar topics written in different moods at different points in time, Pairs of Poems offers a variety of perspectives on subjects as diverse as nature, love, history, and politics.

"With an often politically satiric voice, Pairs of Poems embraces freeways and oceans, warehouse stores and forests, urban parks and picketers. In these twenty-two pairings, F.I. Goldhaber's images move easily from the domestic to the celestial, from a cat's small nose-smudges left on a window to the moon 'marked with sleep lines' at dawn. This collection is the candid record of a seasoned writer who, when faced with 'plot roadblocks,' turns to a 'steamy hot shower,' wondering with wit '...how any good prose/was written before/running water.'"

Oregon Poet Laureate Emerita Paulann Petersen
Author of *The Wild Awake* and *Blood-Silk*

"The title *Pairs of Poems* gives the reader the key to enjoying this book. Each numbered section features two poems about similar themes written in different moods. I love the poet's use of colorful language and the accessibility of the ideas to even a non-poet like me. The poet writes with equal pathos and sly humor about our current political morass and nature."

Marlene Howard
Co-owner/publisher Media Weavers press
Co-founder Oregon Writers Colony

As a reporter, editor, business writer, and marketing communications consultant, F.I. Goldhaber produced news stories, feature articles, essays, editorial columns, and reviews for newspapers, corporations, governments, and non-profits in five states. Now, her poems, short stories, novelettes, essays, and reviews appear in paper, electronic, and audio magazines, ezines, newspapers, calendars, and anthologies. She published seven erotic novels and novellas under another name.

In addition, F.I. shares her words at events in Portland, Seattle, Salem, Keizer and on the radio. She appeared at venues such as Wordstock, Oregon Literary Review, PDX SynesthiA, bookstores, libraries, and community colleges; gives presentations on subjects as diverse as marketing, writing erotica, and building volunteer organizations; and taught Introduction to Indie Publishing at Portland Community College and as a weekend intensive.

http://goldhaber.net/poetry.php

F.I. Goldhaber

Pairs of Poems

Examining various facets of our relationships
with the world and the people around us.

Pairs of Poems

Second Edition
Political Poetry Publishing
ISBN: 978-1-937839-26-0

Political Poetry Publishing
an imprint of Fantastic Worlds Publishing
http://fantasticworldspublishing.com/home.php
P.O. Box 19963
Portland OR 97280

First published electronically by Uncial Press,
an imprint of GCT, Inc.

Contents

Dedication

Dedicated to my parents, Beverly and Jerome Goldhaber
who have always nurtured the poet within.

F.I. Goldhaber

I.

Getting Ready

She slides out of her
mud-splattered Jeep,
straightens her knee-length,
black skirt, adjusts

her panty hose waist.
She runs her fingers
through her long, straight hair
and picks cat hairs from

the white sleeveless blouse.
Reaching inside
for the tailored blue
jacket she slips it

on despite the day's
heat. With bag on
shoulder, she checks her
earrings and marches

in sensible shoes
across asphalt,
steeling herself for the
interview ahead.

Early Morning Commute

Wind whips through my hair.
Asphalt slips away beneath my tires.
The mountain looms large in my vision,

filling my windshield with serenity.
The hulking beauty of Pele sleeping
makes it almost possible to ignore

the tailgaters, low-flying objects
darting in and out of lanes, and SUVs
that pull in front of me only to slow down.

I fight the urge to drive off seeking
unknown trails, mountain vistas and
force the car toward the cubicle trap exit.

II.

Corporations

Cellular One, Ford, U-Haul
Verizon, AT&T, American Express,
Hewlett Packard, U.S. West, MCI.

Corporate behemoths who have
crossed me, refused to do the right thing,
ignored the fair and just complaint.

I took you all on. I know who to call.
I know where to write. I use my words to battle
those who routinely abuse consumers.

FCC, FTC, SEC, PUC.
AG's Office of Consumer Fraud.
Familiar with the government alphabet soup,

I enlist their aid: for the threat of regulators
gets your attention. I work my way up from
supervisor to VP to CEO. Understanding corporate

structure--how to read annual reports--helps
pave the way. I count my victories
in dollars returned, letters of apology, payments made.

Shopping

You can judge
an establishment's offering
by the tone
of the bumper stickers
on the cars in the parking lot

and which petitions
you are asked to sign
as you approach the entrance.

And does a vendor for
the newspaper of the street,
that supports
the homeless, offer
the publication out in front?

If not, do you present
your hard-won dollars
to the wrong purveyor?

III.

Consumer Temple

Welcome to the warehouse, temple
of consumer excess. Fill your carts
with ten-pound boxes of sugar
cereal, hundred-pound bags of flour.
Batteries by the dozens; soap
in ten-gallon jugs too big to lift.

Enough food fills the shelves to feed
a small country, but it parades out
the doors for the SUVs to
swallow while shoppers waddle through the
exit sucking in pizza, ice
cream, and hot dogs too big for the buns.

Wallet Politics

Put your wallet where your politics are.
You railing against Halliburton and
the war in Iraq and Afghanistan;
you complaining you can't find a job that
pays you enough to take care of your kids;
you upset by the lack of health care here;
you shop at Wal-Mart?

But, you say, goods at the other stores cost
so much more; you would have to drive further;
they have everything you need in one store.
Put your wallet where your politics are.
Pay attention to the stores where you shop.
Do you know where their merchandise comes from?
China? India?

Are their toys covered in lead? How many
children lost fingers making those sneakers
earning a dollar a day in sweatshops?
How can you spend money at a store that
destroys local business, deflates wages;
whose employees are eligible for
food stamps, Medicaid?

(continued)

Wallet Politics (continued)

Can you justify saving your money
when you know it comes at such a high price?
Whose pocket do you pick when you choose the
cheapest source? And which politicians will
get campaign contributions from such firms?
Anyone you'd vote for, who represents
what *you* believe in?

IV.

On the Street

I walk by the panhandlers under the freeway
with their hand-lettered cardboard signs aimed at
drivers slowing down to make the turn off the ramps.

I pull my milk crate--attached with bungee cords
to an old luggage cart--filled with newspapers for
recycle or groceries disguised in worn canvas bags.

The mendicants glare at me. They never ask me
for money, for they think I am one of them
eking out a living collecting rubbish to sell.

Others avert their eyes as they cross my path
eager to avoid a crazy, destitute, homeless woman
who might ask for their spare change.

They can't fathom, as they maneuver their groceries
the few yards that separate them from their SUVs,
that I just prefer to walk the mile from home to store.

Signs of the Times

He stands on the street
corner, leaning against
the wooden stake
that holds his employer's
message to the passing hordes.

In between cigarettes,
he sleeps on his feet,
swaying slightly in the
carbon monoxide-laced breeze.

Across four lanes of traffic,
his colleague dances and
waves to the passing cars.
At the end of the day they both
collect the same paycheck.

F.I. Goldhaber

V.

The Mall

The shopping mall barricades
itself from me and the walk
with densely planted shrubs
and endless rows of parked cars.

Pedestrians are not welcome
here and take their lives in hand
attempting to navigate
in through vehicle access points.

They've painted paths
bright yellow leading into
the cavernous altars of
the god of consumerism.

When I leave, drivers
follow me halfway down the aisle;
speed past as I keep walking,
looking for a closer parking spot.

Drive Thru

I walk down the avenue
drive-thrus lining the road on
either side. Coffee here in
myriad flavors, tacos,

fried chicken, hamburgers, dry
cleaning, pharmaceuticals,
donuts, and even money,
all available without

leaving your car. SUVs,
sedans, and pickup trucks line
up six and ten deep spewing
fumes from fossil fuels and their

engines' heat to warm the globe.
They idle for a quarter
hour or more rather than just
park their cars and walk inside.

VI.

Refuge

Fir trees pierce the cloudless sky
sheltering the meadow from
the traffic throttling by.
High tension wires interspersed

among the branches conspire
with automobile engines
to dispel the illusion
of solitude. A ringing

cell phone from the parking lot
increases the encroachment
of civilization. But
then a hawk floating on the

thermals glides over the tree
tops and returns my mind to
enjoying this refuge of
nature within the city.

Interruption

I sit under the
sprawling oak branches
distracted by a
rustling no human

could make. Something small
drops next to my chair
and I peer through the
leaves until I see

bushy tail and bright
eyes of the squirrel
feasting on the ripe
acorns. Confronted,

he scuttles to the
ground and bounds across
the grass to a tree
further away from

interlopers. I
return to my book,
but a bit of a
smile stays on my lips.

VII.

Leaves

Brittle and brown a leaf
scitters across the parking lot.
First one, then another, then

three dance in the breeze and
snicker against the asphalt.
The wind picks up and sends

them whirling about to rest
against the curb and bask
in the fading autumn sun.

The rain and the leaf
blower will chase them
all away tomorrow.

Acorns

Acorns ripe in oak
outside my window invite
squirrels, jays to feast.

F.I. Goldhaber

VIII.

Kitty Television

Her eyes dart about and
follow the dancing leaves.
As they swirl in the wind
outside the window,
her nose presses up
against the glass
of the patio door.

Does she wonder
what strange creatures
cavort outside her world
and whether they would
taste good if she caught one?
The bottom of the glass
is covered with tiny nose prints.

Autumn

The skies open and autumn rains
wash away the summer sun.
Others lament warm days and blue skies gone.

Summer brought for me only a broken heart,
no hiking over rocky trails, no skating
wooded paths, nor paddling murky rivers.

I missed the festivals, the fairs;
concerts in the park; walks along beaches,
and climbs to wild flower-filled meadows.

Lost in my grief,
autumn rains reflect my mood, and
relieve the guilt of a wasted Oregon summer.

IX.

Rain

Acorns crunch under
foot. Leaves turn to red and gold.
When will the rains start?

Brooks

Brooks do not babble.
Skipping over boulders and
rocks, they chatter, sing,
whisper, roar, and gurgle.
But, they really don't babble.

X.

Bobcat

With tufted ears he strides
from the trees and saunters
along the fence through
the verdant green of wide backyards.

The narrow corridor between
house and fence offers him
a moment of safety until
he meets the suburban cul-de-sac.

Surrounded now by houses,
the yearling, with no prior
experience of human habitat,
slowly turns his head from side to side.

He maintains his sovereign
demeanor, but reverses his steps;
wanders back to security
offered by the shelter of the woods.

The Cougar

I walk out to meet you in the darkness
leaving the lights of the subdivision behind
and stumble when pavement turns to dirt path.
I blink trying to see through the trees in starlight.

Will you find me wandering amidst the forest
where you hunt for deer and smaller creatures?
Will your hunger drive you to attack
something other than your normal prey?

I only hope that you will bring me down quickly;
a swift death, I do not wish for pain.
But if I give you my body to feed upon,
will they come after you with rifles and shotguns?

Will they ask why the stupid woman wandered
in the forest at night, or will they see you
as a threat to civilization and hunt you down?
I turn back. I cannot risk your life to take mine.

XI.

Suicide

We cannot really ever know
what demons, mental or physical,
make someone decide
life is no longer worth the effort.

We cannot speculate
about the ravages of time
or chemical abuse;
the loss of memory and thought.

We can wonder if a brain
imbalanced caused despair
so acute that death offered
the only relief from pain.

We can mourn the passing, and
rail against a culture that puts
stigma on but does not treat
depression; denies death with dignity.

But we must try to remember
contributions made, the life
that was shared, and not harbor
anger for the one who left us.

Tears

My heart is full of tears, but I can't cry.
Not for myself. My emotions drain
into my words and the characters I
write. For them I feel joy, pain, arousal.
For them I can smile, cheer, sob.

For myself, nothing.
I see the pain in my life, I just can't
weep for it. For I am the pillar of
tragedy and I must not weaken.

One friend had to quit her job.
She broke up with her boyfriend.
Another's lover betrayed her.
A third starts chemo next month.
A fourth is dying. A fifth just buried her son.
A sixth talks to me of committing suicide.

All of them confide in me. I must promise
I will not share their pain with any other.
They all turn to me for advice,
for consolation, for strength.
If I show my weakness, I can't bolster them.

(continued)

Tears (continued)

My characters bring tears to my eyes,
laughter to my throat, softness to my thoughts.
But the fortitude I offer my friends
drains away my capacity to
experience my own emotions.

My heart is full of tears, but I cannot cry.

XII.

Fellow Travelers

We each have taken
different paths
to recognize
we cannot make the journey alone.
For a short while,
we have traveled
together the difficult road to recovery.

Some of us paid
a horrid price
because we did not
reach this understanding sooner.
Others suffered less,
but still see the abyss
that will swallow us if we can't learn new ways.

We helped each other
over rough
spots in the road.
Though now our paths part,
and we lose that support,
our spirits have intertwined.
We will never forget our time together.

Jim

"I can't come to the meetings anymore," she said.
"Jim needs chemo and radiation."

My mouth fumbled with the questions.
"It's in his lungs. Oh, and it's spread to his bones."

She's married to a dead man.
Does she even know that?

Suddenly my own troubles seem so petty,
the illnesses I battle each day insignificant.

"There's always someone worse off
than you," a one-time lover said.

Is it wrong to allow their misery
to mitigate my own?

XIII.

Betrayal

My words spill out
on the page, exposing
my heart and mind.

I share my words
with the world, but only
when I've weighed each

one to make sure
it is the perfect choice
to reveal my

thoughts. For more than
a quarter century
I have earned my

way in this world
with words. She stole my words;
words not ready

for the world to
see. Words that should have brought
money appeared

on her blog for
all to read. I mourn the
loss of my words.

Words

I keep words.
Kind words, hateful words.
Long discussions of
philosophy I
don't understand, and
can't accept.

Long after
the correspondents
have disappeared from
my life I still have
their words. Megabytes
of words.

Sometimes I
steal them for stories;
use them when someone
I've forgotten turns
up again. Mostly,
I just keep words.

XIV.

Shower Notes

Once someone asked me
why I needed a
computer to write.
Shakespeare composed with
quill pen on parchment
he taunted me. But,
I do not question
how someone could work
in long hand. Though my
brain won't function that
way, I understand.

Instead, I wonder
how any good prose
was written before
running water. My
most formidable
plot roadblocks, toughest
character problems,
get resolved with the
water cascading
over me in my
steamy, hot shower.

Photographer

You observe the world
through camera's lens.
You study the focal
point, aperture,
composition. You
frame the shot, measure
the light. Do you see
the faces of those
you shoot before
you process your film?

F.I. Goldhaber

XV.

Waiting

In the dark night I
pace the tracks, straining
to hear the whistle.

The sharp whistle of
the train that should have
arrived hours ago.

Wondering if the
boy even boarded
or I wait for naught.

The station's bright lights
beckon. But no one's
there. Only taxis.

Their engines run, and
cigarette smoke wafts
from drivers' windows.

I call the Amtrak
information line
for the sixteenth time.

Tragedy

The headlines screech of
tragedy, the new
bride left to mourn.

Freak accident kills
three tourists, halfway
across the globe.

Two Americans,
tsk, we're meant to say.
How very sad.

No names mentioned in
the brief blurb, so I
don't learn until

weeks later that his
mother is a friend
of mine. Small world.

XVI.

I Cry Alone

Their tears dampen the
fabric of my shirt.
I will wrap my arms
around their shoulders,
stroke their hair, help them
all work through their grief.

When someone breaks my
heart, I cry alone.
I won't share my pain
because that makes me
seem vulnerable.
I hide my wounds, my

tears wet only my
pillow. I'll not let
even he who caused
my distress learn he
pierced my defenses.
So, I cry alone.

Tissue

Soft, white fibers
gather my tears,
collect my grief,
catch my sneezes,
accept my sniffles.

Together they wipe
the sweat from my brow,
swallow my pain,
and remove chocolate
from the corner of my mouth.

F.I. Goldhaber

XVII.

Custom Cut

I would have cut myself
from cloth that you would wear,
but you've lost interest
in garments made from me.

You seek the perfect suit
at common ready-made racks,
where you will never find
the custom cut you need.

I shall discover style
that works for me, knowing
that if you come to shop
you'll find it doesn't fit.

Online Dating

The dropdown menu fails to offer a choice
that describes a body cursed by age.
I'm fit, but carry a few extra pounds.
I'm average, but certain places wobble.
I choose "I'll tell you later," knowing
that will scare away more than a few.

Men inundate younger women
with requests for correspondence--
let's meet for coffee, dinner, sex.
Older, and you must take the initiative.
They insist on a photograph,
see grey hair, and stop corresponding.

F.I. Goldhaber

XVIII.

Drifting

Each day I drift
further away from you.
The tether to my heart
slithered by your feet.
You did not bend to grab it.

So my lifeboat
slips, silent, through
the waters as it makes
its way to a world
that does not include you.

The rope floats
in the water, almost
too far away for you
to grasp. Soon it will be
out of reach, forever.

The Waves

They say the tide doesn't come rolling in;
that the waves move up and down.
I know what I see: the pounding
surf inexorably moving toward the shore.

I pause to capture a memory
and the salt water washes over my boots,
kissing my feet with cold before
I can run across the sand.

I watch the cresting waves, the scattered spray,
the sand sculpting, stone polishing water.
Knowing my words will never do its power justice,
I put away my pad and walk on.

XIX.

Romance

The wind whispers across
the water and nudges
the teak and mahogany
craft across the sound.

Cannons boom as sailors
commemorate the glory,
forgetting the blood and scurvy.

They remember the polished wood
and shining brass; never mention
rotten food, missing teeth,
welts blistered on skin by the cat.

Obsession

He hangs on the line, using his weight
to haul sail toward azure sky.
For a moment the nylon flaps in the breeze.
Then it catches the wind and heels the boat to
starboard.

The bow slices through the waves
and skyscrapers shrink to Lego size.

The snow-covered mountain towers behind us,
though we still remember summer's heat.
The haze from burning fossil fuels softens
the edges, blurring our view of the slopes.

Water splashes across the bow
and tourists squeal with delight.

F.I. Goldhaber

XX.

Dreams

Flashes of film
flit through my head.

Snippets of dream
spin my brain from

one bizarre image
to another. My thoughts

race about; bounce off
each other; careen

through the miasma of
my mind 'til I wake.

I lie in bed, exhausted
from the night's exertions.

Dawn Stroll

The mottled white orb hangs low in the sky
lighting the turbulent waters below.
The familiar face looks different here.
Marked with sleep lines, perhaps, across her brow.

The sky around her, tinged with pink and blue,
prepares to greet her brighter sister.
The waves thunder toward packed, wet sand,
smooth enough to reflect the clouds' colors.

They lap at the feet of early risers, who clutch
coffee, until the moon dips behind
fog that conceals the edge of the sky.
Carving a path across the sand, salt water

crawls up to meet the fresh that trickles from
the distant mountains. The gulls know
I've food in hand. They don't skitter away at
my approach but come near enough to beg.

F.I. Goldhaber

XXI.

Winds of Change

Nestled in the once safe valley
we listen to dire predictions
warning us of hurricane-force
winds never experienced here

before. Now the gale tears at the house
trying to rip away flimsy
shingles and brittle siding. The
current White House resident would

have us believe that climate change
does not concern us. But I see
drought become commonplace in the
lush valley and fires develop

into a ritual every
summer extending into fall.
I read of melting glaciers, of
starving polar bears, of islands

that disappear into the sea.
But, I only need listen to
the wind to know the truth of what
we`ve done to this world where we live.

Wind Poems

The wind races
around the house,
inspiring us both.

He writes the slam
poetry of
the young. He talks

of how he finds
comfort in the
wind. Homeowner,

I worry 'bout
lost shingles and
torn siding. I

think how global
warming caused this
horrific wind.

F.I. Goldhaber

XXII.

Lincoln was a Republican

If honest Abe had come to Oregon
to serve as Governor in forty-nine
how differently would our world have evolved?
Would corporations have gained the power

to corrupt the government? Would the man
elected instead to the White House have
antagonized the south and then fought to
preserve the union, trying to keep two

disparate cultures/economies
connected? Would all red states now belong
to the CSA? Without Texas as
spring board would Connecticut-born GW

have stolen two elections? Would we fight
now in Iraq or would 9/11
never have happened 'cause Haliburton
would have no power? Would the slaves in the

south have revolted against white owners,
taking possession of the land they had
worked for centuries, perhaps with support
from a northern neighbor with states of blue.

Oppression

U.S. citizenship
will endanger your health.
In the republic where
we live, the rich govern
the poor. Did someone fool
you into believing
the U.S.A. is a
democracy? Never.

In France, the government
fears the people. Afraid
of protests, parliament
provides health care for all.
Thirty-five hour work weeks,
month-long vacations, and
free education keep
citizens off the streets.

(continued)

Oppression (continued)

In the U.S., people
fear their own government.
Saddled with college debt,
one medical crisis,
even just one paycheck
away from homelessness.
We live in terror of
losing jobs, getting sick.

Even employed, the odds
don't favor access to
health care. And hospitals
routinely dump those who
don't have insurance on
the sidewalk in front of
the mission or send them
off to die somewhere else.

We started the ball of
democracy rolling,
but they kept it in play.
Their citizens live free;
ours demoralized and
too frightened to protest.
Educated, healthy
folk are hard to govern.

Keep them debt-ridden, sick,
ignorant, and poor and
they'll never cause trouble.
One percent own eighty
percent of the world's wealth.
Politicians do not
represent the people,
just the corporations.

(continued)

F.I. Goldhaber

Oppression (continued)

Instead of fixing the
system to meet the needs
of the citizens, they
manage the people to
fit the faulty system.
Keep people hopeless and
pessimistic and you've
no worries 'bout their votes.

If the poor voted for
those who represented
their interests instead
of who corporations
plastered all over the
boob tube, we would have a
revolution unlike
anything seen before.

Democracy is a
radical idea.
It gives power to those
who have no money. A
healthy, educated
nation benefits us
all. Will we ever see
anything like it here?

Jerry Falwell tried to
convince us the attacks
of 9/11 were
god's wrath for allowing
the homosexual
agenda to prevail.
If you read his bible --
the one about Jesus

not the one written by
the Jews -- one could say the
tragedy punished us
for the way we treat our
poor. For Jesus said he
will judge nations by how
well they care for their weak
and sick. We won't do well.

Acknowledgments

The following poems have previously appeared in these publications: "Getting Ready," *The Rambler Magazine*; "The Mall," Sacred Fools Press' *Appleseeds* anthology; "Winds of Change," *New Verse News*; "Interruption," "Waiting," "Early Morning Commute," and "On the Street," *Long Story Short*; "Rain," *3Lights Gallery*; "Brooks," *On A Narrow Windowsill by Form.Reborn*; "Dawn Stroll," Oregon Writer's Colony *In Our Own Voices* anthology; "Fellow Travelers," "Signs of the Times," "Dreams," "Betrayal," and "Corporations," *Humdinger Literary E-zine*; "Consumer Temple," *protestpoems.org*; "Dawn Stroll" and "Romance," *NW Women's Journal*; The Cougar," "Jim," "Online Dating," and "Autumn," *Bridges to Nowhere*.